SOLDIERS SHINE

BY SHARONLYN SILER, RN

Poems dedicated to America
"ONE NATION UNDER GOD"

RoseDog 🐾 Books

PITTSBURGH, PENNSYLVANIA 15222

The contents of this work including, but not limited to, the accuracy of events, people, and places depicted; opinions expressed; permission to use previously published materials included; and any advice given or actions advocated are solely the responsibility of the author, who assumes all liability for said work and indemnifies the publisher against any claims stemming from publication of the work.

ISBN: 978-0-8059-8980-9

Printed in the United States of America

First Printing

For information or to order additional books, please write:
RoseDog Books
701 Smithfield St.
Third Floor
Pittsburgh, PA 15222
U.S.A.
1-800-834-1803
Or visit our web site and
on-line bookstore at www.rosedogbookstore.com

CONTENTS

Represent

Represent...3

Nine One Won 4

Bush 5

A Lesson of a True Leader 6

Home Run...7

Courage 8

A Special Thanks to the United States Military

The Branch 10

Civilian 11

"Mini" Men..12

Brass 13

BuckUp 14

Army Green 15

Mean Machine Army 16

Next to None...17

Air Force Ace 18

Rock Steady (Parris Island) 19

Boot Camp Marine (Momma's Boy) 20

A Warrior 21

Jar Head 22

DAWG 23

Hero Hero 24

Misery Loves Company 25

One Marine's Prayer...26

On Guard..27

Peace Be Still 28

The Heart of America

Loose Letters 30

Kick Back Guy/ Kick Back Girl............................31

Never Lie 32

March 33

A Part of Me 34

One Sun, One Moon, One Love 35

Baby Marine 36
Daddy Don't you Worry 37
Angel..38
Our Eyes 39
Unconditional Like 40
Beyond Beautiful 41
Mission Accomplished 42
Read Between the Lines 43
Do it with You..44
Secret Affair 45
A Penny..46
Can Christmas Come? 47
Christmas Fight 48
A Christmas Kiss 49
Easy Chair...50
If Tears Could Talk 51
Sealed 52
Mountain in My Mind 53
Alone..54
Fence..55
See Saw..56
Depression...57
Who..58
The Comforter...59
Death Lost to Love 60
Rose..61
Define the Rose...62
Real 63

Dedicated to Our United States Veterans

Welcome Home..66
Lights Out 67
Memories 68
Stay in Touch 69
The Wall 70
Soldiers Shine 71

Represent

REPRESENT

Stars shall forever represent,
Our flag and our country and all it has meant.
Illuminating with strength, hope and pride,
A beacon of light, to aid and to guide.
Raising your standards so that all will see,
Your light so fair, over a Nation that's free.
Stripes shall too forever abound,
In a Nation so faithful where God's grace is found.
Stretch forth your truth across the land
Seeking justice and equality for every man.
Stars and Stripes together represent
In War a Flag both tattered and rent.
For the cause of freedom our Flag was torn,
But through its suffering a Nation was born.
Forever together **Stars and Stripes** will be,
A symbol of freedom, for you and for me.

Represent the United States
Its blessings of freedom
For the world to appreciate

NINE ONE WON

The first one won is love for our people.
We stand one nation under God.
The second won is our peace.
We pledge allegiance as we trod.
The third, we are indivisible.
We stand together hand in hand.
The fourth won is our justice.
We fight for freedom for every man.
The fifth is our common defense.
We protect and keep our Homeland secure.
The sixth won is the general welfare.
We establish a democracy that is pure.
The seventh is our courage it's in our hearts.
We are a part of the Home of The Brave.
The eighth is our faith.
We trust and believe our nation God will save.
The ninth one won is our freedom
In this we can all have pride.
These nine were paid for with blood.
And for these nine so many have died.

BUSH

Webster defines the "Bush" with great respect,
To support, mark or shelter is its main object.
It provides security, as each leaf connects,
The "Bush" will surely nurture the land it protects.

The "Bush" will lie low protecting its ground,
Intensely defending all the land it surrounds.
Fervor and strength in the "Bush" does abound,
Find a "Bush" and security will be found.

A LESSON OF A TRUE LEADER

A lesson of a true leader
Is not in the win or lose of the fight.
The lesson is in the challenge.
Face the wrong and make it right.
A true leader is not influenced
by the followers who shout, Turn back!
A true leader holds his position, he remains prepared
for the impending attack.
Often standing alone a true leader will never waver or flinch.
He knows that a battle is not won
With leaps and bounds but inch by inch.
His followers often can't see as far as the tips of their noses.
His followers don't often agree
Ask Martin Luther, Ask Lincoln, Ask Moses.
The lesson of a true leader is not in the lose or win.
The lesson learned by all is the courage it takes to defend.

HOME RUN

Baseball, hot dogs, and apple pie.
It's time to wake up,
wipe the sleep from your eyes.
Sweet land of liberty, the American dream
Can be obtained if you play on our team.
Are you fair and square?
Do you play without error?
Are you for us or against us?
Do you play without terror?
We stand our ground. We cover our bases.
We protect our homeland
with respect for ALL races.
Our bases stay loaded, we stick to our guns.
We will never strike out,
we only hit home runs.
With liberty and justice, we stand tall.
When it comes to equality, we're fair to all.
Our homebase we protect with an iron fist.

Our team plays together....
AGAINST TERRORISTS!

COURAGE

Where were you when we cried
and needed you most?
We lost the lives of our loved ones
on the Gulf Coast.
No words could ever describe
the pain and devastation.
The destruction of property,
it was an awful situation.
No one mind could comprehend
or two eyes have ever seen
The nightmare that blew in
and destroyed New Orleans.
All of America stood by
as they watched with disbelief.
A storm that destroyed came in like a thief.
Hearing the cries of the children,
and seeing the death of women and men.
Touched the hearts of Americans
it cut straight through our skin.
The tender lives of our people
were swept away by the flood.
With each went a promise
Paid for with blood.
In times of such tribulation
on this promise we all can lean.
Look up and have courage, read John 3:16.

**A Special Thanks to the
United States Military**

THE BRANCH

Army, Navy, Air Force, Marines
United for Freedom
And all that it means.
Rooted and grounded, pruned to perfection
Each branch spanning outward
In every direction.

When a "leaf" takes a fall
The branches grow stronger
As they pause to recall
That one "leaf" lives no longer.

Each branch grows stronger through service and labor,
As it reaches to shelter its country, its neighbor.
Each branch independent, yet united in aim
Motivated, dedicated, and believing the same.
Army, Navy, Air force, Marines,
United for Freedom
And all that it means.

CIVILIAN

I woke up this morning and I realized
That I am free because of you guys.
I rolled out of bed then down on my knees.
I prayed to God, "Protect our guys please."
Then I hurried about with my daily affairs,
Realizing I'm free because someone else cares.
Someone out there is fighting for me
Fighting for our country so that we all remain free.

"MINI" MEN

"Mini" men play it safe,
Never taking that daring jump.
"Mini" men never take a risk,
Never make it over the hump.
"Mini" men never try,
To make a go of it,
They give excuses as to why,
But the truth is, they just quit.
"Mini" men will never rise
To the top or to the occasion.
"Mini" men never take the lead
Through coercion or persuasion.
"Mini" men cannot be trusted
To play a "Major" part.
They leave you feeling scorn and disgusted,
Because they have no heart.
"Mini" men will never be great,
This is the reason why…
"Mini" men would rather give up,
Before they even try.

BRASS

Recognize that gentleman,
Acknowledge him passing by.
Stop, salute and shout "Yes Sir!"
He's no ordinary guy.
No sir, he's not just polished,
He shines like a brand new silver dollar.
You can tell he's somethin' special,
By the brass that's on his collar.
Yet he does not take for granted,
All the men in his command.
He gives them all he has to give,
He's an Officer and Gentleman.

BUCK UP

Pull pride up by its boot straps.
Get ready to be the best.
Get ready for the attack, never stand back.
Be prepared to be better than the rest.
Dig guts out of your hind-site.
Pour "never give up" in your cup.
If you want to win learn to defend.
Go ARMY ! Go ahead and buck up!

ARMY GREEN

You must confess, we're better than the best.
The best that you've ever seen.
If you're looking to grow
then you should know.
Your best bet is to go army green.
You will admit that it takes true grit
Strength and a mind that is keen.
Uncle Sam wants **YOU.**
What are you going to do?
Go ahead and go Army Green!

MEAN MACHINE **ARMY**

The color Army Green
Stands for "Mean Machine".
If Uncle Sam Wants You,
And you're not sure what to do.
Here's the answer to your question.
(This is an order not a suggestion)
Join the Army wear the "Suit",
Become a "Mean Machine" Recruit.
When you put on Army Green
You become part of the team,
You're unafraid to show your might,
And you're ready for the fight.
Not just a fight for fighting's sake,
But the fight that courage takes.
No "Wishy-Washys" or "In Betweens"
Can wear the honored Army Green.
Who we are? The Mean Machine
The United States Army decked in Green.

NEXT TO NONE

We never say "never",
It's a negative reply.
When you ask us to jump,
We ask you, "how high?
We never use the phrases,
"No way" or "No can do".
If you ask if we will.
We'll say, "YES" 'til it's through.
We never say, "Never",
"No can do" or "No way",
When the others leave early,
We are willing to stay.
We never say, "Never"
Cause we're number one
We are the NAVY, Second to None!

AIR FORCE
ACE

With highly trained precision,
We never stray off course.
With courage and true decision,
We fly high with fighting force.
Determined to be number one,
We strive to be the Best.
We are the bona fide "Top Gun",
We are better than the rest.
Enforcers of sky, land and sea,
No fear, No turning back.
We confront the enemy
Before they can attack.
When it comes to "First in Flight"
The Air Force sets the pace.
And if you want the job done right,
Send the Air Force, The Ace!

ROCK STEADY
(PARRIS ISLAND)

Rock and rock don't make bone.
To get hard rock, you must have stone.
To make a Marine it takes a clean slate.
About 13 weeks it takes to create.
Brick upon brick around the clock.
It takes hard drive to make hard rock.
Bit by bit, down to the bone
Break men down; make men grown.
Next knock hard rock off his feet.
Then pick him up; he's now concrete.
Ready to roll this rock is heavy.
A Lean Marine ready to rock,
Rock steady.

BOOT CAMP MARINE
(MOMMA'S BOY)

My son is not made of iron and steel,
He's only flesh and bone.
I don't want my son to die out there,
So don't leave my son alone.
My son he said he runs all day,
Out in the rain and heat.
Does he get the time to pray out there?
Does he have the time to eat?
My son wrote home, and said to me,
I miss you, Dad and Sis.
I wrote him back and I said to him,
"Son, why did you enlist?"
He replied, with words that I shall not forget,
"Mom, it is my duty, and it's you I must protect."
P.S. Sergeant,
I don't want my son to know
I'm writing you this letter.
He would be so angry,
But it makes me feel much better.
I hope I haven't bothered you,
Or put you on the spot.
I'm just a Mom who's worried sick
For the only son I've got.

A WARRIOR

How do you make a Marine out of a man?
You start with the statement, YES I CAN!
Make the man shout out loud and clear
until he becomes a warrior without any fear.
Train the warrior, prepare him for war.
Make him MORE than a man and BETTER than before.
Take him to the limit, push him past the end.
Pull "I can't" out and put "I can" in.
Run the man at a faster pace.
Remove ALL defeat and put win in its place.
Not many men make warriors, believe me it's true.
To become a Marine, most don't have a clue.
A few men they make it PAST the man mark.
They walk in to the light and out of the dark.
It's in the light a warriors true colors are seen.
He is now among The FEW, The PROUD, The MARINES.

JAR HEAD

Jarheads are empty because we dig down deep.
We know the cost of courage never sells out cheap.
We give our all asking for nothing in return.
The reward of respect a true warrior will always earn.
We reach down deep and we pour our all out.
We are the water in the driest drought.
When the going gets tough and no one else is around.
A jarhead will keep searching until the answers are found.
When all else fails, a way we will find.
All the answers are found in the warrior's mind.
When most give up, Jarheads dig in.
Giving our all because that's how we win.
Jarheads are empty because we give our all.
When courage is needed, we answer the call.

DAWG

Who is YOUR Dawg?
Do you recognize his bark?
Does YOUR Dawg walk with you —
Through the storm and through the dark?
Will YOUR Dawg come on command?
Is Your Dawg ready to attack?
Does YOUR Dawg really give a damn?
When the rest don't give a jack?
Does YOUR Dawg take pride—
In the job he's trained to do?
Does he tuck his tail and hide?
Or is he off the chain, like you?
Is YOUR Dawg unlike no other?
In the light and in the dark,
Do you call YOUR Dawg Your Brother?
Do you recognize his bark?

<u>HE</u>RO **HER**O

Webster defines the word **"Hero"**
As being a warrior, courageous and bold.
<u>**He**</u> is the masculine warrior
and the <u>**Her**</u> is the warrior of gold.
Webster defines the word "Gold" as a beautiful and precious thing.
A yellow precious metal worn by a king or queen.
Webster defines the word "**He**," referring to the male or men.
The **Her** in the word Hero means female or feminine.
The **Zero** at the end of her**o** means nothing a warrior will regret.
Nothing we are not proud of the gold is the standard we set.
The real meaning of a true hero
is not found in a dictionary or book.
If you want to discover the real meaning.
A Marine is where you should look.

MISERY LOVES COMPANY

Misery loves Company,
When I'm down they're tried and true.
When Misery makes me tired,
My Company pulls me through.
Strong shoulders to lean on,
And a back that's sturdy too.
This Company that I'm a part of,
Are a proud and mighty "Few".
Standing side by side together,
On Misery's battleground;
In the midst of Misery's weather,
No better shelter can be found.
You are my Homies cool and tight,
My Dawgs who have my back.
When Enemy Misery comes out at night,
My Company Dawgs attack.
At times Misery takes my joy away,
And often cuts me to the bone;
But thank God for my Company,
That will not let me stand alone.

ONE MARINE'S PRAYER

Here I am again God, one Marine, one heart.
I don't know where to begin God,
I don't know just where to start.
I guess I'll start as usual, by stating my request.
But first let me say Thank You,
Before I say what's on my chest.
I do not have directions,
To find the peace I'm searching for.
But if I'm going to find it,
I believe you are the door.
Here I am again God,
You said, "If I'd knock, you'd let me in,"
So I stand here knocking at Your Door,
One Marine, One Heart, One Friend.

ON GUARD

Never again will I let you down,
Discipline is my defense.
With an eagle eye, I question why,
And uncover your pretense.
In plain eye view - I study you,
Never revealing to you my game.
It's all an act, as I gather the facts.
While treating you just the same.
You will never catch me latent again,
The past was a lesson learned hard.
Now I'm sleeping with one eye open
So Beware, this Soldier's On Guard!

PEACE BE STILL

Surrounded by the enemy without a place to escape.
My back is against the wall and
I can't cut through the red tape.
Sending out a signal searching high and low.
Trying to find my peace of mind and a quiet place to go.
Several times I've tried to find the words for a prayer.
I searched my mind and then my heart
but the words are never there.
Surrounded by the enemy my life and spirit
they try so hard to kill.
With my back against the wall I heard a voice say,
"Peace Be Still".

Mark 4:39

The Heart of America

LOOSE LETTERS

Loose letters were lying on the floor
when I walked in the door today.
I could hardly recall how each got there
But I knew that's where they were going to stay.
I peaked in the slot of my mailbox
to see if your letter was there.
I stuck my hand in, the letter was thin
and I knew that you really did care.
I sat on the floor, propped against the
door and started to read my letter.
I read it again and again and again
and it made my heart feel much better.
My day is not complete
without loose letters at my feet.
I sit on the floor and I read.
I read them all over and over again
because its your love that I need.

KICK BACK
GUY

Kick back and relax.
Take it easy in your chair.
Close your eyes, now imagine I am there.
Place both hands behind your head
Breathe me in, and remember what I said.
I said that I would always be your girl.
And that you mean more to me than anything in this world.
Take a deep breath. Now breathe me in slow.
Hold me in forever and never let me go.
Breathe me in, feel me inside of you.
With each breath I breathe, you're inside me too.

KICK BACK
GIRL

Kick back and relax
Take it easy in your chair.
Close your eyes, now imagine I am there.
Place both hands behind your head
Breathe me in, and remember what I said.
I said that I would always be your guy.
You mean the world to me and that's no lie
Take a deep breath. Now breathe me in slow.
Hold me in forever and never let me go.
Breathe me in. Feel me inside of you.
With each breath I breathe, you're inside me too.

NEVER LIE

This morning when I woke up I called your name out loud.
I dreamed that I had lost you in the middle of a crowd.
I realized it was just a dream and I began to cry,
You said I'd never lose you, and I know you'd never lie.
The dream it felt so real to me, I could almost feel your touch.
Desperately pushing through the crowd, wanting you so much.
I kept yelling, "Why'd you leave me, Why, my darling, why?"
You shouted through the crowd to me and said, "You'd never lie".
⸳ You said for me to wait right there, that you were on your way
I kept crying out, "Don't leave me please, my darling stay".
In my dream you said to me, hold on and not to cry,
But I had this awful feeling, and my feelings never lie.
I was so happy to wake up and find it was a dream.
To find that it was make-believe, as real as it did seem.
When reflecting on the dream a tear falls from my eye.
As I recalled the day you said to me, "You would never lie".

MARCH

Its only when I think of you,
I gather the strength to march right through.
My boots are filled with dust and sand.
Tough thick calluses are in my hands.
My skin is dark, scorched by the sun.
My shoulders hurt,
from the weight of my gun.
It's only after I think of you,
I find the strength to march right through.
Sometimes my mind can't take the strain.
The cost the loss, brings so much pain.
Each day seems longer than the day before.
I need your love to march through this war.

A PART OF ME

A part of me is across the sea and I know that I must go on.
I can feel my soul pouring through the hole
where my heart once did belong.
Can you feel my heart, it's with you.
Do you know that my spirit is there?
Every moment that I'm not with you,
our love we still will share.
I can feel your spirit behind me,
like a shadow, you are so near.
I remember that you are with me.
I can hear your voice so clear.
You said that you would always love me,
and soon you'll be coming back.
You promised that nothing could separate us,
not even the war in Iraq.

ONE SUN, ONE MOON, ONE LOVE

So many miles so far away
You're in the night; I'm in the day.
So many miles, so far apart, I'm in your dreams,
You're in my heart.
So many miles across the sea
We share One Sun that we both see.
So let the Sun that kisses your face
Remind you of my warm embrace.
I hope that I'll be home real soon,
But until then, we'll share One Moon.
Let that Moon recite to you
Sweet poetry, of love so true.
May the shadow of the Moon's caress
Frame your lovely silhouette.
Let Sunlight's fingers touch your hair
Let Moonlight's arms hold you with care.
Let us thank the Lord above
For One Sun, One Moon, One Endless Love.

BABY MARINE

I'm growing inside my mommy.
Tucked down safe and tight.
I love to kick around, I hope my mommy feels alright.
The night I came alive, I could hear my daddy say,
Take care of my baby. And then he went away.
Sometimes I can hear my mommy talking on the telephone.
She said " A part of daddy's inside, and she is not alone".
I can't wait to see my daddy's face
when he takes a look at me!
A baby girl or a baby boy, he doesn't know what I will be.
Its not time yet for me to come out, I'm as little as a bean.
I look just like my mommy with the blood of a Marine.

DADDY DON'T YOU WORRY

Dear Daddy,
Don't you worry I'm doing my very best.
Mom she said she's proud of me
and for me she feels so blessed.
Daddy I'm doing all the things you showed me how to do.
I'm checking all the doors at night
and studying hard in school.
Daddy don't you worry
I'm doing all the things you said.
I turn out all the lights at night
and I'm making up my bed.
Daddy I'm not worried,
I'm big and strong and rough.
I'm growing up to be like you,
smart and tough and stuff.
Daddy don't you worry.
I'm keeping an eye on Baby Sis.
Daddy come home in a hurry
because Dad it's you I miss.

ANGEL

So still, so silent, so soft, so sincere.
When a little child prays the angels stand near.
Dear Angel,
My mother is so sad, my brother is sad too.
My daddy's not at home and I don't know what to do.
My friend she told me to kneel on my knees.
Fold my hands and say
" Pretty Angel Please".
Please Mr. Angel take God this letter.
Ask him to make my mother and brother feel better.
After you are done please fly to Iraq,
pick up my daddy and please bring him back.
Mr. Angel you don't know me, I am just a little girl
who loves her daddy more than anything in this world.
Mr. Angel, thank you for listening to me again.
Thank you for my family, I love you.
Amen

OUR EYES

We share a secret among us guys.
You can find this secret in our eyes.
When our endurance is put to the test
What is hidden in our eyes gives us rest.
Our days begin before the sun does rise.
And we rise with that look in our eyes.
The look that says, there's a job to be done,
There's a battle to fight and a war to be won.
Before one day ends another one starts;
The secret in our eyes gives hope to our hearts
With all the things that we fight through
Our eyes tell the secret, our eyes miss you.

UNCONDITIONAL LIKE

Love is my promise forever to you.
To forever be patient, to forever be true.
Love is a contract I have signed in my mind
To bear all things and forever be kind.
My promise to love you, I keep in my heart.
It will always be kept there, it was there from the start.
My promise I stand on when times don't seem right.
For instance the times when we argue or fight.
My promise is the anchor when I want to sail.
The hole in my bucket when I want to bail.
My promise is the brake on my bike for the hike.
My love is unconditional unlike his friend like.

BEYOND BEAUTIFUL

No one but you would ever do what you did for me.
You went past the task I didn't have to ask.
My need only you could see. I was left high and dry
and only you would try. You went beyond, you held on to my hand.
No one but you could ever pull me through
And only you tried to understand. What can I say?
I can't ever repay. I can't start. Where do I begin?
There's no one like you. You're beyond beautiful.
May God bless you and keep you my friend.

MISSION ACCOMPLISHED

I am on a mission
That must be kept hush, hush.
If I give up my position
She'll discover I have a crush.
I'm laying out my plan.
First there's A, and then there's B
Plan A is my Playa Playa Plan
Plan B is simply, me.
Plan A may work for other guys
They act so suave and cool
But when I try to use Plan A
I look just like a fool.
So I've resorted to Plan B
A humble, decent man
I'll let her see the honest me
I'll do the best I can.
I think this Plan is working out
I should have used it all the time
Honesty is what it's all about
Mission Accomplished, the Girl is mine.

READ BETWEEN THE LINES

I am sending you this letter.
To let you know that I am yours.
I want you to know that when you get home
I'm opening up all my doors.
I'm waiting every day for your soon return.
I want you to know when you get home I'll let my oven burn.
My house is not a home.
I'm living here all alone.
I'm letting you know that I am yours.
You can ring my telephone.
I'm sending you this letter to let you know I care.
I want you to know that when you get home
You can rock in My rocking chair.
I want you to read my heart, my soul and my mind.
When you get home I'm opening the door.
Go ahead and read between the lines.

DO IT WITH YOU

I dropped a pot on my baby toe.
I wish I could do it like you.
The kids said they wanted pizza instead
After I burned up the stew.
I burned a hole in my good white shirt.
I wish I could do it like you.
I wanted to look nice in my white.
But instead I'm wearing dark blue.
I went to buy grocery but I spent too much.
I wish I could do it like you.
I bought ten turkeys and such and such
Where the money went, I don't have a clue.
I helped the kids with their homework last night.
I wish I could do it like you.
The teacher called and said it was not right.
I should just help and not their homework to do.
If I could have you here right now
I would kiss you from head to toe.
I would wish that I could do it with you
And I would never let you go.

SECRET AFFAIR

Go ahead and face the fact
You just cannot commit.
Creeping and sneaking behind her back
And that's just the half of it.
Your words are saying one thing
But your eyes are saying another.
You promise love and a wedding ring
But I'm just your secret lover.
You have someone at home.
Does she believe your lies?
Is she listening to your words?
Is she looking at your eyes?
It's written on your face,
The words you're speaking you don't mean.
Go ahead and tell the truth.
With me, you just cannot be seen.

A PENNY

Take time to think of little things that you are thankful for.
I'm sure if you can think of one,
you will somehow think of more.
Take time to set aside some time
to reflect on yesterdays gone by.
Remember the good times and the bad,
it will almost make you cry.
Take time to smile and lend a hand
to those who pass your way.
Remember the times that someone smiled,
it helped to make your day.
Take time to share what you have
with those that have and have not.
Remember the times that you
were in need or have you somehow forgot.
Take time to be thankful for being free
in this land of good and plenty.
Remember the price our Veterans paid.
Our prayers don't cost a penny.

CAN CHRISTMAS COME?

My little son who was sucking his thumb
Said, "Mommy when can Christmas come?"
I looked at him, with his little grin and
I asked, "Where did that come from"?
I said it's June and much to soon,
To think of Christmas my son.
He took his thumb out and said with a pout,
"Mommy you're just no fun."
He started to cry and then asked me
"Why can't Christmas come in June?"
He said, "I want my present!
I want my daddy to come home soon."
I felt a tear drop and my heart stop
As these words I did carefully say,
"Christmas has come and your present my son
Is Daddy's love for you everyday."

CHRISTMAS FIGHT

My father brought home a Christmas tree
after Christmas day.
My mother she cried when she saw him outside
she said, "Honey are you feeling okay?"
My father said, "I'm sorry I forgot about the kids and you."
My mother said "I know you are sorry,
I also know your love is true."
My father said " I got drunk on Christmas
and I stayed out gambling all night.
My money was stolen, my jaw is swollen,
I must have been in a fight."
My mother she took my dads hand,
she bathed him and fixed him dinner.
I learned on that winter night that love makes a sinner a winner.

A CHRISTMAS KISS

Christmas is supposed to be the best holiday of the year.
I know my heart should really be filled with lots of Christmas cheer.
I would forego this Christmas, believe me, this is true.
I would gladly skip the 25th to spend the 26th with you.
I'd give up gifts this Christmas for just one hug or kiss.
Just to have you close to me, this Christmas I would miss.
So Soldier if you hear me, wherever you may be
Don't send me any presents, put my kiss beneath the tree.

EASY CHAIR

A folded flag rests on my mantel above the fireplace.
Beside it is your picture; I hold often, I embrace.
I was sitting in your easy chair that day they brought the news.
What the sergeant had to say to me.
My heart still does refuse.
I couldn't believe what I heard.
I closed my eyes, I covered my ears.
My mind went blank I felt faint.
My eyes filled with tears.
I felt that I was in a dream.

I asked, is it true? Is it so?
I can't believe that you are gone.
Why did you have to go?
I would do anything to have you here again.
The price, your life. You gave your all.
Our nation to defend.
Life is not always easy. It is often so unfair.
But right now I'll sit and reminisce in your easy chair.

IF TEARS COULD TALK

If tears could talk what would they say?
You're not alone, why don't you pray?
If you could listen and listen close
They would say, God cares the most.
If tears could talk what would they say?
Hold on tight, helps on the way.
If you are feeling alone and blue
The pain that you're feeling he felt too.
If tears could talk, what would they say?
Your broken heart he'll mend today.
Just open the word and take a look.
All the comfort you need is in His book.
Now hold your head up,
he will wipe the tears from your face.
For every tear that you shed, he will put love in its place.
So go ahead and cry, let it all out.
That's what tears are for and love is about.

SEALED

Continuation of my frustration seems too much for me to share.
The heavy burdens of my situation to unload seems so unfair.
Never ending, forever growing are the problems inside my cage.
Deep depression forever digging deeper holes that cause me rage.
Tossing and turning in the nighttime. To wake to problems, real.
Burdens heavy, never ending never told.
My lips are sealed.

MOUNTAIN IN MY MIND

I'm climbing a mountain in my mind.
This mountain it stands all alone.
My mountain is covered with years of tears.
So very hard with a heart made of stone.
I reached up to conquer what I feared most.
Take hold of the mountain in my mind.
I struggled to take hold of fears uncontrolled
pressing upward for the peace I would find.
I struggled so long, trying to hold on.
Too afraid to look back or look down.
To look down is to recall the pain of it all,
How it feels to be low to the ground.
Day after day I'll continue to pray.
And keep climbing towards the sky.
I'll keep climbing, I can't stop.
I need to reach the top.
To find the answers, my mind questions why.

ALONE

The walls around my mind keep me locked inside myself.
I can't find the keys to unlock and escape my own mental health.
Deeper I fall into this hole that forever pulls me down.
I'm completely alone and abandoned.
I feel no one is around.
Looking up at the walls of loneliness
They are made of thick black stone.
This hole I'm in is dark and deep and I am left here all alone.
I try to crawl out but the walls are slick,
I have nothing to hold on to.
I cry inside, I feel I've died and there is nothing that I can do.
Deeper I fall into this hole that forever pulls me down.
My only hope is a glimmer of light
that I have somehow looked up and found.

FENCE

There is a fence around my heart,
Painted black and locked with chains.
No one can get through to my heart
For my fence keeps out the pain.

This fence I made with purpose and plan
I hammered each post very deep
I placed them close together
So Ole Man Trouble cannot peep.

I keep my heart barricaded
From all the cares of life.
Shielded from sorrow and worry
Hidden from all pain and strife.

I keep my heart fenced away
Letting no one in to see.
Who I am or how I feel
Or the secrets I hide in me.

I keep my heart locked away
In a safe place, I call my own.
Yet, this fence I've built has kept me
So lost and all alone.

SEE SAW

I stopped to smell the roses, but guess what?
They all stank.
I tried to keep my boat a float, but guess what?
My boat sank.
I tried to look on the bright side, but guess what?
The lights were out.
I tried to make a run for it, but guess what?
It ran out.
See, I saw the truth of it.
What seems ^{up} is sometimes $_{down}$.
When you're standing on your head…
A smile is just a frown.

DEPRESSION

Too many times I have been blind
with my eyes so full of tears.
I couldn't see ahead of me,
I couldn't face my fears.
I dug a hole within my soul,
I crawled down deep inside.
No one knows I'm hiding here,
and a part of me has died.
So many times I'm so alone
even with the world around.
I'm not a part of their laughter
I can hardly hear a sound.
I feel my life take motion like
a slow locomotive train.
I stay on track, not looking back
the past holds too much pain.
Memories of my broken dreams
all pieces of my confession.
Tiny fragile parts of my broken heart
All add to my depression.

WHO?

Who can take this pain away?
A part of me has died.
I've cried so many tears.
I have nothing left inside.
Who can fix my broken heart?
I can't go on like this.
My mind remembers everything
And It's you my heart does miss.
Who has made a promise to me
that we would never die?
If we believe in His name
we would never have to cry.
Who? His name is Jesus.
He holds the keys to life and death.
He gives us life forever more.
Our life is in His breath.

THE COMFORTER

Too many Soldiers' mothers
Are left all alone to cry.
Left alone and without answers
And hearts that question why.
To whom do the mothers turn to?
Who'll dry the tears from their dear eyes?
Who is there to bear the pain?
Who hears her groans and sighs?
Too many Soldiers' mothers
Hold stories too painful to tell.
Alone without the answers.
They must live a private hell.
Who will comfort the mothers?
The Three combined make One.
The Father sends His Love
Through The Holy Spirit and His Son.

"And God will wipe away every tear from their eyes;
There shall be no more death. Nor sorrow, nor crying.
There shall be no more pain,
For the former things have passed away."

Revelation 21:1-4

DEATH LOST TO LOVE

Death stood dark and angry clutching a sickle in his hand.
He proclaimed to his opponent Love, "I've murdered every man."
Death said to Love, "It looks like every man has met his doom."
Love said to Death, "Where is your sting? Go look inside the tomb."
Death cried out with an awful shout,
"Who has stolen him from the grave!"
Love said to death "The King has
risen and his children he rose to save.
Death cried aloud, "I own them, and they belong to me!"
Love said, "You are defeated, I now claim the Victory!"

Mark Chapter 16

ROSE

Rose how beautiful the meaning to see
Deep red the blood that was shed for me.
How beautiful the meaning each flower to bloom
a single petal rolled back like the stone from his tomb.
How beautiful each thorn on the stem to be found
Placed on the Rose to be made for a crown.
How beautiful the fragrance the scent from the flower.
A sweet reminder, no man knows the hour.
No one knows, no not one
The day the father will send the Son.
How beautiful the meaning
The petals fade and close.
The Flower died
but on the third day He rose.

DEFINE THE ROSE

Define the Rose and define true beauty…
The Scent: His Spirit Given Sweetly to me.
Deep Red: His blood that was shed for me.
The Petals: His wounds that bled for me.
The Thorns: The crown He wore for me.
The Stem: The Back that bore the cross for me.

How beautiful the Scent of the flower,
A fragrant reminder of His mighty power;
How beautiful is its color, deep red
A visual reminder of the blood that was shed.
Consider the way each petal recedes
Like a wound that dries after it bleeds.
How finely honed is the Rose's thorn,
A painful symbol of the Crown that was worn;
How yielding the stem and yet so strong
Like our Savior, carrying the cross for so long.
How wonderful was the Flower that died,
Nails in His hands and a wound in His Side;
"It is finished" He cried. As His eyes wept and closed.
Thank God for the love and the passion of the Rose.

REAL

I won't deny this loneliness that only God understands
I feel as though I can't go on and I don't believe I can.
To say I miss you is not enough to describe this pain I feel.
The days are long, it all seems wrong, can this all be real?
Real is the love we shared when you were here and living.
Now my life and heart are cold and very unforgiving.
Real is the life we shared, now what is it worth?
I can't replace this precious love with anything on earth.
At times you seem so close that I feel your love all through me.
It helps me survive, though you're not alive, real love is the key.

Dedicated to Our United States Veterans

WELCOME HOME

Will they recognize the pain in my eyes?
Will they feel the stillness in my soul?
Will they see the hurt in me?
Will they know how my heart has grown cold?
I question why I'm still alive.
It's only a miracle I've survived.
I will never be the same; I'm broken and lame.
My life is shattered. Tell me, why should I try?

We recognize the pain in your eyes.
We feel the stillness in your soul.
We can see the hurt in you and we know
that your heart has grown cold.
When we remember you,
It's your courage that shines through.
When we reflect on the great debt unpaid
We are humbled beyond measure.
Your sacrifice we do treasure.
We humbly thank you,
for the sacrifice that you made.

LIGHTS OUT

Some day my life will be over.
My lights will soon be out.
Right now I'll live, my all I'll give.
Because that's what life is all about.
Yesterday day is gone forever.
And tomorrow is on the run.
Today I'll live, laugh, and forgive.
As if my life has just begun.
Yesterday remembers my past.
And tomorrow doesn't know a thing.
Now is the time to live it up,
it's life's song I'm trying to sing.
Today is a blank sheet of paper
Waiting for me to right.
Right all the wrongs of yesterday.
For tomorrow might turn out my lights.

MEMORIES

Memories of so many lost.
The tears, the hurt, the shame.
My mind remembers everything.
Will I ever be the same?
My mind can't stand the thought of it.
Shallow graves with out a name.
I remember all of it.
Will I ever be the same?
Whistling missiles, bursting bombs.
I can't escape the sound.
I try to erase the memories.
Like a dog, they chase they hound.
Loud cries, passers by, gunshots that ring out loud.
My mind remembers everything.
The death, the grave the shroud.
Memories of an awful war.
My life, the price no gain.
My mind remembers everything.
I will never be the same.

STAY IN TOUCH

What about my life?
I only have a few good years left to live.
I gave them all I have.
Now I have nothing left to give.
What about my dreams?
Can I give just one a shot?
I gave them all I had.
Yes, I gave them all I've got.
What about my time.
I have little left to grow.
My time was spent with them.
Now I have no place to go.
What about my cares?
I cared for them so much.
Will someone care for me?
I'll have to see.
I'll stay in touch.

THE WALL

Let it be known, etch it in stone.
Engrave their names on the wall.
Never forget the sacrifice of our Vets.
Remember to reflect on it all.
Remember me because you are free.
Remember the land I died for.
Remember to respect our native land
and keep it forever secure.
Keep your eyes on the sky.
Keep your head held high.
Place our flag in the forefront of your mind.
Remember the red, the blood that was shed.
True blue soldiers like stars they shine.

SOLDIERS SHINE

Soldiers stand next to the stars.
That's why they shine so bright.
There is always a soldier standing guard,
Keeping watch all through the night.
Remember the fight, respect the light.
To our native land always be true.
Remember the red, the blood that was shed.
Pure white stars and soldiers true blue.
Lift your head and remember the light
It shines at such a great cost.
A soldier stood by and kept watch for you
For this light, his life was lost.
The stars seem often so far away.
And so often we may forget.
Each star remember fought for freedom for you.
A price paid for with the life of a Vet.